THE SMALL MAGIC

LIFE-CHANGING LESSONS WE LEARN FROM CHILDREN

MARIA HORRIGAN

"'Sometimes,' said Pooh, 'the smallest things take up the most room in your heart.'"

—A. A. Milne

To children everywhere.
May you never stop believing in magic.

The Small Magic

Copyright © 2023 Maria Horrigan

ISBN Hardback: 979-8-9885792-1-2
ISBN Paperback: 979-8-9885792-0-5
ISBN eBook: 979-8-9885792-2-9

Cover design by Maria Horrigan

Interior design: Andy Meaden meadencreative.com

Edited by Hannah Kates

All drawings featured throughout the book were created by children of the families the author has worked with.

CONTENTS

Introduction	1
Creativity	5
Excitement	11
Letting Go of the Need for Control	17
Present in the Moment	25
Be Bold and Beautiful	31
The Perfect in the Imperfection	37
Forgiveness	43
Compassion	47
Cultivate Joy	51
Resilience	57
Vulnerability	61
Consciously Curious	67
Perspective	71
Don't Overthink It	75
Magic	79
Final Thoughts	83
Acknowledgements	85
About the Author	89

Introduction

It's the year 2005. The walls around us seem to get smaller and smaller as my younger sister Olivia and I *patiently* wait for Mom to call. "I'm bored," Olivia says. If it weren't for the seemingly endless supply of crackers and juice cups in the doctors' lounge, Mom might have had to search the halls for two girls running around like chickens with their heads cut off. But, since those halls were hospital wings, we figured we'd better not test our luck.

As much as we enjoyed gorging ourselves on snacks, it was always more exciting to waddle behind Mom, following her from room to room as she made her hospital rounds. From the postpartum moms with their new infants to the grandfathers who never failed to have their best jokes prepared for us, the faces of both young and old lit up like Christmas Trees when we entered the room. At that young age, it never dawned on us to consider what it was that made these patients so happy.

Now, eighteen years later, I understand children's remarkable ability to uplift the spirits of those around them. Their infectious laughter and playfulness can ignite sparks of joy and comfort in life's most challenging circumstances. All that time spent in hospital wings as a child later taught me the greatest lesson of all: miracles follow children wherever they go.

When I wasn't pole vaulting over bars, running to class, or traveling the country for the next track meet, I spent early mornings, three days a week, working jobs that brought me peace amid my hectic college life. After watching two young boys for most of my teenage years, it was an easy decision to settle on babysitting as a part-time job that quickly became my main source of income.

As I delved further into my psychology degree, I was introduced to a child psychology lab that focused on reading and comprehension among elementary-aged students. My peers and I spent copious hours at schools, testing children one-on-one to better understand the ways they decipher information. Those two years of weekly interactions with children in schools showed me how much I enjoyed studying how children think. It was then that I decided my heart truly belonged to working with children.

After graduation, I jumped at the opportunity to attend the University of Dayton to pursue their master's program in school psychology. I remember the genuine excitement that surrounded me during that transition. But after figuring out that a career in school psychology wasn't going to allow me to spend as much time with children as I'd hoped, I decided being a school psychologist wasn't in the cards for me. Leaving a graduate program surrounded by people who wanted to devote their life to helping children was one of the hardest decisions I've ever had to make. By that time, I knew I wanted to make a difference in kids' lives, but I wasn't yet sure how to do so. What I did know was that I wanted to interact with children as much as possible. *What job can I get* right now *that would put me in front of children all day without having to go back to school?* I thought. *Ah, yes. Nanny it is.*

Over the last five years my job as a full-time nanny has given me a front-row seat to joy every single day. My days are filled with singing, dancing, games, and all sorts of silliness, and the older I get, the more I realize how much of that silliness gets lost as we grow up.

Each chapter in this book highlights moments of inspiration sparked by the children I've cared for. Their sense of innocence, wonderment, and originality drives me to be a better person. The experiences I share in this book are meant to remind you of the magic we knew as children and how easy it is to access—if only we remember to look for it. I hope you see parts of yourself and the children you know inside these stories. Take the lessons with you into your day-to-day life. And for those of you with children of your own, I hope that in addition to everything you teach your little ones (and the infinite lessons they'll teach you), you find a way to share the wonder that shines in their eyes.

CREATIVITY

*The real magic wand
is the child's own mind.*

—Jose Ortega y Gasset

With the amount of time I spend playing with children, I often joke that I need to remind myself to snap back into reality when I return to the real world. However, I oftentimes wish I could stay in their worlds forever.

A pair of siblings I know well, Ethan and Elsa, *live* for putting on puppet shows. From princes rescuing princesses to dragons raiding villages—and their favorite, Dorothy and the Tin Man. Given the number of times I've had a front row seat to their version of *The Wizard of Oz*, I have to remind myself that monkeys don't actually fly!

As I quietly watch them perform, I'm inspired by the amount of work they put into these plays: picking out the colorful outfits, ensuring each scene is perfectly staged, and offering the audience (a.k.a. me) refreshments at each break. They perform these shows simply for the fun of it—for that feeling of excitement only the power of imagination can bring.

I'm sure many of you have witnessed a similar form of child-designed entertainment, all the while wishing you could absorb just a sliver of that energy into yourself. Taking care of children makes me want to be a part of the magic, but sometimes, it's downright exhausting. Yet, even on the days when playing along seems almost impossible, I still walk away utterly amazed by the creative ambition children possess. Why is it that so much of that joyful, impassioned energy perishes as we age?

In this fast-paced, unpredictable, yet extraordinarily innovative world we live in, the drive to harness creative energy is equally desirable and intimidating. But somewhere along the path to adulthood, creativity becomes mandated. Almost like imagination gets replaced with obligation.

Here's the silver lining: creativity is available to all of us. We can all harness our inner magic, and I promise you, it's still in there. The secret is to recognize there is magic in the mundane… but only for those of us who choose to seek it out.

The copious hours I've spent crafting with the kids I work with have reignited my passion for art. The messiness of finger painting, the families of puppets, and the piles of Play-Doh all inspire me to create projects during my own free time. I now find myself painting at home in the evenings and on weekends.

Although crafting may not spark your interest, I encourage you to find ways to explore creativity for yourself or with the children in your life. Sit down and write a poem for your significant other or create a scavenger hunt for you and your children to complete together. Re-do your kitchen backsplash or plant new flowers in your front yard. Ask your child to design a game and play it together. It's in these moments that we tap back into that childlike nature and rediscover the power of creativity. You might even consider writing a book or something…

Excitement

There are no seven wonders of the world in the eyes of a child. There are seven million.

—Walt Streightiff

I spent my early childhood living on a golf course, though, surprisingly, I never found one golf ball in my backyard during the entire seven years I spent in that house. My older brother Michael and I did, however, find countless golf balls in the pond behind my neighbor's house. If you consider yourself a golfer, you know how much golf balls sell for nowadays. So, naturally, my dad, being a decent golfer himself, would encourage my siblings and me to dive into the golf course ponds, hoping that we'd rake out a few Titleists he could clean up to use on the course. And boy, did we find them! We found so many balls that instead of putting up a pop-up lemonade stand like most kids in the neighborhood, we created our own niche selling restored golf balls.

Every Sunday, Michael and I would pull the wagon full of golf-ball-loaded Ziploc bags to our designated turn on the cart path. We each had multiple baggies labeled with the brand name and the cost for each set. We were like the Horrigan concession cart children, only instead of selling beer, we offered cleaned-up Pro V1s. The golfers adored us! We had the locals grinning from ear to ear.

When I think of this story, I can still feel the genuine excitement we had on those days, even if we only sold a couple of balls. It helps remind me how intriguing the world is to little ones. They're endlessly interested in everything and often have zero hesitation when offered the chance to try something new.

We so often see children overflow with glee about the simplest things. It makes me stop and think. How often do we get excited like that? Why, as adults, does that excitement seem to fade so quickly or to escape us completely? When was the moment we grew timid about being blatantly ecstatic about something?

In the seriousness of our adult lives, it can be challenging to garner excitement on a regular basis. But here's something that worked for me when I found my enthusiasm waning.

Shortly after finishing college, I spent several months living in Lemoore, a town in central California almost completely surrounded by cattle farms. Discovering fun and exciting avenues in such a place was more challenging than I expected, but I also knew it was vital if I wanted to maintain my sanity. The neighboring town hosted a farmers' market every Sunday. At first, my then-fiancé Ryan and I simply enjoyed attending, until I thought, *Wait a minute. I could be a part of this.* Two weeks later, I returned to the famers' market with a California seller's permit, a display rack I made from old closet shelves, and the canvas paintings I'd been crafting over the years.

I never expected to show, let alone sell, my artwork that year—but wow, am I glad I did. I've since created a website and continue to sell my artwork online in addition to my local farmers' market. The excitement I felt setting up my table that first Sunday morning in California and every time since is quite like the feeling I had on that golf course twenty years ago. Adventurous and exhilarating.

If you find yourself searching for that excitement in your life, be willing to try something new. When was the last time you did something for the first time? It could be anything from visiting the history museum down the street, joining a book club or even starting your own. Test out a pair of rollerblades or send someone a funny postcard. Maybe you love to cook. How fun would it be to have a cook-off with your older kids, your spouse, your neighbors, or your friends—winner gets to choose the game for family fun night! It could even be recreating a specific activity you loved to do as a kid and sharing it with those around you.

Spend a few moments making a list of experiences you feel drawn to or maybe even apprehensive about. Once a month, pick an activity from the list, find the time to schedule it, and commit to making it happen.

Because younger children have not yet

developed a "comfort zone," most things are new and uncomfortable to them. I think that is why they experience so much excitement. They demonstrate that going out of our comfort zone is natural and invigorating. They also remind us that it's okay to jump up and down every now and then. My hope is that the more you choose to adventure, the more excitement you'll experience. And if you can't find anyone who will live in that excitement with you, the children around you will—every single time.

Letting Go of the Need for Control

*We grow old chasing the truths
we knew as children.*

—Atticus

It's amusing to hear the range of opinions people have (whether they have children of their own or not) regarding kids and those who work with them. The two views I commonly get are, "that must be a piece of cake" or "that sounds like the equivalent of pulling my hair out." The truth is that a day watching kids usually ends up somewhere in the middle. Every day with children is wildly different, but for me, that's what makes it most exciting.

I love my job because it's incredibly rare to get bored. Some days I show up and am greeted with the biggest hugs and smiles. Other times, I walk into screams loud enough to deafen the neighbors. Yes, most days I return home utterly exhausted, and sometimes I think I'm going to lose my ever-loving mind. But then I see a toddler hug a baby doll like it's the last time they'll ever hug anything, and I'm reminded of why I choose to surround myself with little hearts. Those moments of pure love that burst from the hearts of children illustrate why we're all here.

Every summer, I do my best to plan a trip to the zoo. I assume many of you have also made this a tradition for your families, and if so, you know it's a trip that requires some serious preparation. A zoo day by yourself alone in the heat of summer can be exhausting, let alone with multiple children tagging along. Waters, snacks, toys, hats, sunscreen… The list seems never-ending, and what I've come to realize (and have definitely experienced myself) is that this overload of preparation can create a serious need for control.

Making sure that everything goes according to plan can turn a trip that's meant to be fun into a trip filled with stress. Here's an example from my zoo escapades that has shown me the difference between planning and controlling.

At every zoo exhibit, there are typically two types of caregivers: those that follow their plan so closely they overlook the main reason for the trip (to have fun) and those who think of their plan as more of a flexible guideline, meant to change along with the ever-changing whims of the children they accompany. I hear the first caregiver's child say, "I wanna see the giraffes!" Then the caregiver responds with, "Well, we have to see the monkeys first because they're on the way to the giraffes." Nine times out of ten, I see this end with a meltdown in the middle of the aquarium. And for what? Are the monkeys honestly too important to skip?

Two feet away, I hear the second caregiver's child ask, "Can I have my sammich now?" when it's clearly not lunch time. Instead of saying, "No, it's not time to eat yet," that adult realizes that even though an early lunch wasn't part of the day's itinerary, giving the kid that sandwich will save them from a likely tantrum.

Each party in these situations was prepared, and both had a plan going into the day. But their experience at the zoo turned out completely differently.

Society tends to project this illusion that life is predictable and under our control. Being around kids shows you just how untrue this is and can provide you with loads of practice in learning otherwise. It's hard enough trying to control our actions, let alone the actions of little humans who have minds of their own. Regardless of how frustrating it can be, many of us struggle to make room for the joy that lives within the many moments of surprise we encounter every day.

When unanticipated change happens in our lives, the wiring in our brains leads us to stress out, feel disappointment, or even lose control in moments of chaos. What if, instead of getting frustrated in these situations, we embraced the wonder that hides behind the fear of surprise. Instead of feeling bothered by endless folding of living room blankets, you choose to see the happiness those forts bring to a child's heart. No matter how many times Henry throws his food from the highchair, the sound of his laughter that follows is too beautiful to be upset. And although you feel like a zombie walking into the nursery for the fifth time that night, the feeling of that little hand wrapped around your finger is worth a lifetime of no sleep.

One thing I struggle with is releasing control of how my future unfolds. I'll get myself so worked up about finding that perfect apartment, worrying if I said the right thing, or making split-second decisions, fearing another opportunity won't come along. I can drive myself crazy thinking I'm able to control every little detail of my life, and if I somehow fail to attain what I wanted, I'll spend the rest of my day focusing on what I could have done differently instead of acknowledging all the things I did right.

A great way to work on releasing control is to establish touchpoints throughout the day: opening a door, taking a sip of coffee, or seeing a kid walk past you on the street. When you notice these things, ask yourself, *Am I in a controlling state or an allowing state?* If your answer is a controlling state, cue your mind to consciously return to an accepting frame of mind. Remind yourself that not every moment will turn out exactly as you would like it to and all you can do is try your best. Learning to be adaptable to life's curveballs is what enables us to keep our balance. Try not to get stuck on particular outcomes and instead take what the world gives you as what author Gabby Bernstein refers to as "detours in the right direction."[1] This way, you start to accept what you can't control and can more easily notice and enjoy the positive moments along the way.

Going forward, try to release control and adjust accordingly. I promise, you *will* find magic in the unexpected. Once I slowed down enough to see how simple it is for kids to find joy and peace amidst change, the better I became at finding it as well.

---

1 *The Universe Has Your Back: Transform Fear to Faith,* Gabrielle Bernstein, Hay House Inc., 2016

Confidence

I am going Otyin

Christopher H.

- Age 6

PRESENT IN THE MOMENT

In the eyes of a child, you will see the world… as it should be.

—Unknown

One of the perks of living in the city of Savannah is the ease of walking through the many squares and parks with the child I nanny. The distance around thirty-acre Forsyth Park is about one and a half miles, and based on how many times I complete that loop pushing a stroller, I basically accomplish my step count for one week in a single day. One thing to know about Savannah is that there is never a shortage of tourists.

One sunny spring day, Ioné (twenty months) and I were out for our routine stroll. Walking with a toddler around busy streets can be both entertaining and exhausting, and that day Ioné was particularly set on getting to her favorite "Red Bus" café as quickly as possible. As I reminded her clumsy self to look up while she walks, we came upon a group of older tourists admiring a building downtown. In that moment, it would have been quicker to slide through the crowd, but I chose a different route. I knelt down and said to Ioné, "Do you see those people looking at the building? I think we should pause and watch them for a second. What do you think they're looking at? What do you see?" Her eyes lit up with the challenge. That was all it took to become present in that moment.

"Thank you for being patient," a visitor whispered to us as they wrapped up and wandered by.

Imagine yourself walking through the door after an exceptional day at work. All your meetings were productive, someone surprised the office with donuts, and you even landed that client you've been speaking with for months. You're feeling on top of the world. Now imagine yourself eagerly running to your partner or calling your friend to share the news… only when you tell them, you hear rustling over the phone, or you notice your partner glance over to the television as they simply nod along with an obvious lack of engagement. How do you feel? Discouraged? Overlooked? Maybe even frustrated?

Now remember the last time you told a child a story, whether it was a bedtime fairytale or the time you ran the New York City Marathon. Could you see the light fill their eyes or feel their attentiveness to the story? Children practice presence every day; adult duties or anxieties aren't pulling their attention away yet. Every time they sit to color a picture, stop and smell a flower, or get sucked into book, they show us their ease of concentration in the present moment.

Consider your own day-to-day. Are you truly present? Does that same light fill your eyes, or do you fixate on the past and worry about the future? It's incredibly easy to rush through moments that seem insignificant or trivial. With the growing length of our agendas, it can be tempting to run around exhausting ourselves, struggling to accomplish everything at once, or to mentally check out and simply go through the motions.

When you find yourself on autopilot, try taking a break to recenter yourself. Take a walk. Make eye contact and greet the strangers you see. Study the things along your path: nature, people, buses, and buildings. Maybe even stop and smell the roses!

Everybody has to-do lists, but what if we had *to-be* lists? Schedule some uninterrupted time to sit in silence and think about a few adjectives describing how you want to show up in your daily tasks: joyful, optimistic, motivated, or even *present*. When I find myself overthinking or rushing through one task just to get to the next, I remember the way children experience each moment fully. I remind myself to slow down and return to the present moment.

Be Bold and Beautiful

And the dandelion does not stop growing because it is told it's a weed. The dandelion does not care what others see. It says, "One day, they'll be making wishes upon me."

—B. Atkinson

Am I the only person who believes picking outfits for children is significantly more fun than choosing clothes for myself? The possibilities are endless: unicorn shirts, striped stockings, superhero capes, shoes that glow in the dark… I mean, come on. Most of their sunglasses are cuter than mine.

A simple way to experience a fun side of a child's personality is to let them dress themselves. I would often do this nannying on summer days when we had few plans. The girls would race to their closets and choose the most eccentric outfit with little hesitation. Shirts would end up backwards, inside out, and for some reason, the odds of them picking out socks that matched were about a million-to-one.

During the next half hour of, "No I wanna do it!" their personalities are on full display. The combination of colors and patterns (or lack thereof) gives you an insight into the way their minds work. The girls would twirl around until they were dizzy, saying, "Aria, look at how pretty we are." Not once did they need to look in the mirror to believe that statement. They just knew.

How many times have you circled your room trying desperately to pick the perfect outfit? Or made sure your hair looks exactly like that Pinterest post? What if we were all certain about the beauty we possess, regardless of what we wear or the way we look? Let me tell you, young children have absolutely zero doubt about theirs.

It's so unbelievably refreshing. Children possess the incredible power to pull us from our world full of expectations, standards, and trends and push us into their world where creativity and acceptance live and reign freely. The way children so effortlessly shine their light everywhere they go reminds me of *our* freedom to do the same. It's time to retrain ourselves on how to find our beauty, both inside and out.

When I feel unhappy, whether that be about the way I look or the way I feel, I listen to the thoughts that fill my head and sometimes even write them out. Instead of continuing down the path of self-loathing and negative self-talk, I write down the parts of myself I love the most and return to my best self. Try it; you may be surprised at the number of positive qualities you come up with. Keep these written traits where you will see them often: your bedside table or the mirrors in your bathroom. I used to keep mine tucked in the sun visor in my car!

Another way to shift your mindset when you are feeling down is to think about a time a close friend or loved one confided in you about a tough situation or negative feelings. What did you say to them? That the light will come, and they're beautiful no matter what? I think most people, myself included, are better at giving advice to others than taking their own. So the next time you stand in front of the mirror doubting yourself, spin around a couple of times and tell yourself what you would tell your best friend: "Look how beautiful you are!"

(4) NOLA

The Perfect in the Imperfection

Even a broken crayon can still color.

—Random church sign

It was just another Wednesday. I was preparing lunch while the two littles played nicely in the toy room. After cleanup, the three of us were walking upstairs to get ready for naptime when I noticed a few marks on the railing along the steps. Finley continued casually until we got to the top of the steps, then she grabbed my hand and led me to the wall next to the bathroom. "Look, Aria," she said. "I drew you a pitcher."

"Oh," I said. "Well, thank you, Finley, but you know better than to use crayons on the walls."

"I didn't," she replied proudly. "I used marker!"

With the multiple moves I've made around the country in recent years, the number of kids I've worked with has grown considerably. Yet, that first meeting with a new family never fails to excite me. With each home I enter come new personalities and lessons I have yet to learn. Of course, every family I meet has their own special quirks and routines, but one thing that continues to baffle me is the tendency for each of them to apologize for the clutter that invariably blankets the home of a young child.

Our world has created an image of a *perfect* home. One where kitchen floors are spotless, the kids' hair is always brushed, and toy rooms look like Ikea showrooms. Life is messy, and I've seen firsthand how much messier it can get when kids enter the equation. But what some people tend to forget is that the pathway to peace tends to weave straight through the disorder that surrounds us.

What if instead of feeling the need to portray a flawless (un)reality, parents could be honest about how exhausting bath time can be or the fact that the beds are rarely made? Would the world flip upside down if someone found out the kids had McDonald's for dinner last night?

My family was fortunate enough to own a video camera when my three siblings and I were growing up. These tapes mostly captured baptisms, birthday parties, and the occasional temper tantrum—which, ironically, are now incredibly hilarious. The recordings are mainly of events that I'm sure seemed the most memorable at the time, but when we watch them back, the best footage isn't of the *big* moments. It's the sibling-taped videos of our everyday life as kids that remind us of what our childhood was really like. The craziness that's captured in those tapes is comforting. They're filled with silliness: dorky dance routines, arguing over who gets the first piece of cake, wild water balloon fights, and popcorn spills all over the carpet during movie nights. Those are the moments that most accurately represent the *reality* of our lives as children.

Fifteen years ago, ten-year-old Maria was singing into a video camera, and because she didn't have any outside sources to compare herself to, she was *completely* convinced she could win *American Idol.* Today's ten-year-olds are picking out which filters on their phones align with the rest of their media feed. And what's worse: so are their parents.

There seems to be a certain age when a child's relentless innocence succumbs to the pressure of portraying an image deemed adequate by society. Kids today are led to believe they must pick and choose the parts of themselves they see as *perfect* and share only those parts with the world. These children are growing up in an age brimming with virtual judgment, unrealistic expectations, and fabricated identities. Now more than ever, it's imperative to teach kids to love and accept all the quirky, flawed, and beautifully unique parts of themselves. Instead of apologizing for their messes, parents should start saying, "As you can see, my kids made some memories today!"

It saddens me to see that the few early years of a child's life have become the only period where they can be wild, outspoken, bizarre, and ultimately *free.* Young kids never fail to be honest, even when the truth can be embarrassing, brutal, and often incredibly insightful. When was the last time you felt completely free to express yourself or answer a question without fear of judgement?

One fear that's followed me much of my life is the fear of being judged as uninteresting. Sometimes, I hesitate to chime into conversations, thinking my point may in some way lack validity. But when talking with a child, I don't think twice about saying what honestly comes to my mind. Kids have taught me that honesty keeps us interesting. Today, I worry less about giving the perfect answer and more about being myself: a bubbly, blunt, compassionate goofball who just wants everyone in the room to feel like they belong. Staying true to who we are is the real magic. And with every authentic act, our confidence and self-respect grows, knowing we didn't pretend to be someone we're not.

"Deadly Ra~
Desert" He~

FORGIVENESS

*The way we talk to our children becomes
their inner voice.*

—Peggy O'Mara

I once watched a toddler accidentally destroy a massive dollhouse creation that had taken his older sister three hours to complete. It only took his sister three seconds to hug him and say, "I forgive you, Ethan."

In my experience, the younger the child, the quicker they are to apologize, even if that means simply repeating what they're told. In a toddler's world, "I'm sorry" is the get out of jail free card.

Though young children may not fully understand what "I'm sorry" means, they learn that by apologizing, they receive forgiveness. Children crave forgiveness because they feel ashamed that they may have done something wrong, and when they start to understand how good forgiveness feels, they desperately want to share that forgiveness with others. When was the last time you met a young child who could stay upset for longer than ten minutes? It's almost as if their brain contains the secret, *life is too short to hold on to anger for too long.* If only adults were so wise.

Since I grew up in a home where forgiveness was considerably cultivated, forgiving others hasn't been a major stumbling block for me. It's forgiving *myself* that has always been the hardest.

If you're like me, you may neglect or deflect the

negative feelings associated with something you did or didn't do. Eventually, those neglected feelings come up and out into the open, affecting the way we act towards ourselves and others. When this happens, I find it's helpful to think of how children so effortlessly offer forgiveness and remember that I can offer myself the same grace. Instead of pushing those emotions away, I forgive myself for the hurt and move on. I remind myself that every mistake is a lesson added to the library of wisdom within all of us. Every time you forgive yourself or others, you take a step toward a more peaceful mind, like that of a child. Watch closely, and you'll notice how open children are about sharing their feelings. Don't be afraid to accept the things that make us human. Children remind us that past the wall of forgiveness, lies a field of peace. Try following their lead on this one.

COMPASSION

The greatest gift we can give to a person in pain is to hold in our own minds the thought that there is a light beyond this darkness.

—Marianne Williamson

While my time as a nanny has been overwhelmingly amazing, there are downfalls to any job, and for me, this one came as a great sense of loss. It's a unique profession where you're asked to protect a child yet keep them at arm's length to remain professional, a job where you spend more time in someone else's home than in your own. You help lead children to be the best versions of themselves without knowing if you'll see the fruits of your labor because, well… you're simply the nanny. In my experience, nannying has become so much more than a job. It's how I choose to spend most of my time, loving the hearts of children that aren't mine and raising humans I may never see again.

After two full years of ten-hour days, five days a week in the Levering household, tears filled my eyes as I thought about moving across the country in a few short weeks. The four kids scribbled away at their art projects as the youngest, Kylie, came over and started patting my hair.

"Don't cry, Rhya," she said. "It's otay." In that moment, a two-year-old girl showed me more compassion than I was able to show myself.

Think about a time when a child saw you upset and how quick they were able to act with love. They have the beautiful ability to sit with us in discomfort, even when they don't understand it. Children have shown me the power of sitting in silence through times of sorrow—not only with others, but also with ourselves. I think people mostly want to be heard, not told what to do. It can be tempting to throw ourselves into others' situations and ramble about how we would handle things. But instead of shifting the focus onto yourself, try to humbly show up with an open heart and extend as much silent love as you can. The more I noticed how often children show up for us, the easier it became to show up for myself and others.

CULTIVATE JOY

When my daughter was about seven years old, she asked me one day what I did at work. I told her I worked at the college—that my job was to teach people how to draw. She stared back at me, incredulous, and said, "You mean they forgot?"

—Howard Ikemoto

One thing I can die knowing for sure is that the inventor of bubble blowers is an absolute genius. Introducing bubbles to a toddler is like witnessing a magic trick. It's clear the toddler doesn't quite believe what they're seeing, but their brain cannot resist marveling at it. At this age, magic and marvel are still so real. Their innocence lets them believe anything is possible. Watching a child's eyes ignite in awe as they chase little globes of clear magic is one of the most beautiful things in this world.

This past winter, I accompanied Ioné and her mother to the pediatrician for her routine checkup. As we sat in the waiting room full of infant carriers, toys, and crying babies, a little girl no older than two entered the room. Completely uninhibited, she ran in a circle saying hello to everyone in sight, running into chairs and tripping over her shoelaces. The sound of her laughter filled the air, just like the laughter of children chasing bubbles.

Throughout my life, I've come to understand that real, honest joy isn't something that usually falls into your lap. Most of our days are filled with responsibilities, challenges, and uncertainty. The world has come to associate happiness with people, pursuits, or material things, all of which are *outside* of ourselves. As we age, success starts to be measured by our accomplishments and the aspirations we long to achieve in this life. A goal-orientated lifestyle is perfectly commendable, but we mustn't forget that the "play" performed on the road to those goals is equally important.

If you slow down and observe children, they almost always find ways to enjoy the journey on the way to their achievements. Whether it be your daughter's continuous revision as she creates a project for the school science fair or your nephew's innovative vision for his futuristic Lego city, watch as enthusiasm lights up their faces and stimulates their minds. This doesn't just happen at the *completion* of the goal, but all the way through the process. It's their playful nature that supplies them with that infinite supply of energy we all long for.

I've thought long and hard to narrow down the one element all children share that makes them so happy, no matter their age, gender, background, or abilities. This magic component fuels their playfulness, imagination, and joy to a level that's unattainable or maybe even forgotten as we age. This secret ingredient, I've discovered, is the element of *fun*. All kids ever want to do is to have fun. Ask any child out there what their idea of fun is, and they'll have an answer ready quicker than you can read this sentence.

Yes, as a nanny, *fun* is pretty much built into my job description. But what's interesting is that all the time I've spent cultivating fun for others has programmed my mind to seek ways of finding fun in my own everyday life, regardless of whether it's a "good" or "bad" day. When was the last time someone asked you what you like to do for fun? Or better yet, when was the last time you asked yourself?

Occasionally, when I dive into tasks or interactions that I truly don't feel like facing, I go into them focusing on the pile of work I have yet to do or how much time is left before I can escape. This mindset makes me miserable. Trying to rush through that meeting or mindlessly doing laundry strips our capacity to appreciate the process of progress and robs us of enjoying the good moments along the way.

When I catch myself wishing my responsibilities away, I immediately imagine how I could spin the situation to be even the slightest bit fun. Maybe your mother-in-law asks if she can stay at your place to visit the kids over winter break. It can be easy to fixate on the things we'd like to avoid, but imagine if you traded all that energy spent overthinking and instead used it to generate as much enjoyment as possible. Rather than catastrophizing about how those two weeks might unfold, what if you sat down with her and made an event-filled schedule for those two weeks: taking the kids to a hockey game, baking cookies, a trip to the zoo…

The beautiful thing about creating joy is the infectious nature of it. By generating fun for others, you end up taking part in that joy as well. Everybody wins—imagine that!

Seeing kids' remarkable ability to discover joy in every situation encourages me to find joy for myself. Children remind us that we're always meant to experience the world with fun and joyful energy, even in our adulthood.

RESILIENCE

Life is not about how fast you run or how high you climb, but how well you bounce.

—Vivian Komori

A few years ago, I picked up some part-time work at a daycare (yes, I genuinely thought it was a good idea to go straight from nannying four children to a classroom full of one-year-olds). After repeatedly struggling to pronounce the word shoes, a toddler named Elliot eventually added the stubborn word to his rapidly growing vocabulary. Along with shouting the word, he demonstrated his newfound knowledge by waddling around the room, attempting to take everyone's off—including his own. As he approached each of the other kids, I couldn't help but notice the expression of pride on his face as he showed us all proof of his resilience.

When we see a kid succeed at something after struggling, we often think, *Wow. Kids are so resilient!* We're usually eager to share this with them. Their reactions to their own triumphs are wildly entertaining. Young kiddos will flaunt their accomplishments as if they just split the atom. And while it is wildly hilarious to watch them strut with their heads held high, there are plenty of moments beforehand where they could have given up. But in my experience, most kids, even in times of intense struggle, hurdle right over those setbacks, smiling and ready to try again.

As adults, we tend to assess resiliency by how easily or quickly someone bounces back after moments of difficulty or misfortune. "Wow, you bounced back from that breakup pretty quickly!" However, children have shown me that resiliency isn't "bouncing back" as much as "bouncing forwards." The fear of failure tries to convince us success is unattainable. We try something once or twice, and if it doesn't take, we tend to write it off and return to our old mindset. Why? Even if we did fail or struggle in the attempt, didn't we learn at least something from it? Children have a keen ability to focus their attention on alternative routes rather than limitations. With every loss, they still win because they accept it's what necessary for growth—at age four or at age fifty-four. And even though their aspirations to become superheros, fairytale royalty, or their favorite cartoon character may be a bit far-fetched, maybe it's time we bounce *forward* and sprinkle ourselves with a little bit of that fairy dust.

touch down

VULNERABILITY

Children don't say, "I had a hard day, can we talk?" They say, "Will you play with me?"

—Lawrence Cohen

At the time of writing this chapter, I'm finishing up my Master's in Teaching Elementary Education. After two years of completing courses part-time from the comfort of my (many) homes, I was placed into a classroom this spring to observe and teach a few lessons before I begin full-time student teaching in the fall.

I spent the majority of those days watching and learning from the first-grade teacher whose back table became my desk for that month. I don't know if it was because I could fit in the one-foot-tall chairs or because I also ate the little boxes of cereal the students were given each morning for breakfast, but they asked me how old I was probably four times every hour.

Since I'd been spending the past nine months with an eighteen-month-old, it was quite stimulating to enter a room full of seven-year-olds who have one million things to say to anyone who will listen.

"Songbirds sound fancy. I wish I sounded fancy."

"I can't read because I have brain damage right here."

"My sister's room is down the hall next to mine, but my mom and dad's room is downstairs but down the hall downstairs, but I think my grandparents are going to be moving in soon and they're gonna be upstairs but down the hall."

"Why don't we put animal DNA into people in the army?" All I could think was, *Are you from the future?*

And just when I thought I couldn't hear anything more random, one afternoon while helping a young boy complete his reading assignment, he says to me, "Miss, you know, my mom is a scientist, and she says that… Wait, let me look at your eyes. Yep, green. She's a scientist, and she says that people with green eyes are very fun to play with."

I couldn't help but smile. I love kids.

Imagine a continuum of self-confidence and self-doubt. As we grow up, our acceptance of "not knowing" or speaking what is truly on our minds tends to become progressively more fragile. With every error or rejection, our fear of other people's perception grows, whether that be in an academic space or looking like a fool during a game of poker.

Before spending all this time with children, my inner voice would skew toward self-doubt when I entered a room of professionals in a field that wasn't my own. *I don't belong here. What if someone found out how much I don't know about politics?* Why was that my automatic response? Do children do that when they walk into their classrooms? As I got older, it's like a sense of *shame* became associated with being wrong or looking foolish. Why, as a child, is it okay to be curious, when as adults, we're so insecure about not having all the answers?

Think about how normal it is to see children stumble, fail, and make a fool of themselves on a regular basis. Maybe the reason they're so carefree is because half of their day isn't consumed with worry about making a mistake or "acting the part." Children are so truthful about their experiences and knowledge, that it makes you want to share yours with them. They recognize how life is simply a journey of continuous learning, and allow themselves to be vulnerable, even if it's scary.

The adult world has a lot to learn from the vulnerability of children. Try to grow more comfortable with admitting your mistakes. This not only helps to honor your experiences, but it might also encourage others to confidently share their own. Imagine a world where we could all seek and share knowledge as openly and safely as children do, without fear of judgement. That's a world I want to live in.

CONSCIOUSLY CURIOUS

Don't look at your feet to see if you are doing it right. Just dance.

—Anne Lamott

How long has it been since you listened to a seashell? Two weeks? A few months? Ten years?

A few summers ago, I was lucky enough to travel south with a family I'd been nannying for. Many mornings on that trip, the kids and I would jump out of bed at the crack of dawn, throw on our sweatshirts, then slide into our sand-covered flip-flops before racing down the steps to the beach. As we all held our little buckets to fill with treasures, I couldn't help but reminisce on the moments I'd done the same with my own family as a child. The two youngest girls splashed in and out of the water, grabbing as many seashells as their little hands could carry. It didn't matter whether the shell was in perfect condition or if it represented a long, harsh journey. To the girls, each shell had a special story to tell.

Until that trip, I had forgotten how common it is for children to pick up a seashell and instinctively put it to their ear. It had been years since I'd heard the whisper that was once so familiar to me, a sound only children think they're able to decipher. They're endlessly curious about everything they encounter, and as the girls stood on the grainy sand, pushing shells onto my ear, they made me realize it was a sound I sincerely missed.

This story is meant to demonstrate how kids shine a light on the importance of curiosity. Consider your closest relationships, maybe with your life partner, your best friends, or even your parents. Some of those relationships may lack intimacy for a variety of reasons, but I've found that a major element in maintaining strong connections is curiosity. I think most people agree that at the beginning of a new relationship, it's exciting to share your thoughts and desires about everything under the sun: your favorite foods, your passion for yoga, or what character you would choose to be from the Marvel movies. But as we progress in our relationships, our lives get busier as routines set in, and that feeling of curiosity sadly starts to fade. We stop asking those quirky questions—and sharing and learning about ourselves in the process.

A method to shift interactions with those special people in your life is to simply change the way you ask questions. Make sure your questions are *meaningful.* In my experience, vague questions like, "How was your day?" result in a bland response like, "Good, what about you?" nine times out of ten. What was the point of even asking? On the other hand, when I ask precise questions like, "What was something exciting that happened to you today?" it's much easier for that person to recall a specific moment that sparks a deeper conversation.

For children, each new interaction is a miracle, and they see it that way. Try to remember what it was like to be unapologetically interested. And the next time you're at the beach, pick up a seashell and listen for the curiosities from your own childhood. It could tell you something you may be missing.

PERSPECTIVE

*Try to be a rainbow in
someone else's cloud.*

—Maya Angelou

Within the first few weeks of my freshman year at college, I began working for a family with two young kids, Anna and Lyle. Three days a week, I was up before sunrise and off to the Baker household. While their mom ran errands, I would feed the kids, color more pictures than I did in elementary school, and play so much hide-and-seek that, sometimes, I felt like *truly* hiding.

It was in this house that I learned firsthand what a child could teach adults about overcoming difficulties. Anna, who was three years old at the time, had been diagnosed with childhood apraxia just a couple of months before I started working with her. Apraxia is motor speech disorder that can make it difficult for the brain to deliver correct movement instructions to the body. In Anna's case, it hindered her ability to accurately pronounce words. Although I'd grown up in a home where medical terminology was like a second language, I'd never heard of this disorder before meeting Anna.

Anna would regularly work on her speech sounds and exercises. It was fascinating to watch the patience of such a young child during moments she felt misunderstood. While most children Anna's age tend to talk a mile a minute, she would quietly "read" to herself or dress up her baby dolls in all sorts of outfits before rocking them to sleep. She loved sitting by the pond near their house, watching the geese dip in and out of the water. Her quiet gentleness allowed space for me to notice how at peace she was with the cards she'd been dealt. Maybe those tough cards were the exact reason she'd developed such a loving and caring nature. Maybe our greatest adversities can become our greatest strengths.

My mother practiced family medicine in the small town of Bowling Green from the time I was two until I was fifteen. When she was twenty-eight, she was diagnosed with multiple sclerosis right after the birth of my younger sister. Despite knowing her career would never be the same, her M.S. diagnosis completely changed her perspective as a physician. Being able to truly understand what her patients were going through gave her insight that she never could have understood otherwise. It was the very adversity that put her career in jeopardy that ended up making her the best doctor she could be.

When I pause to consider the challenges in my life and in the lives of those around me, I recognize the gifts that lay beyond the doors of difficulty. Watching children face challenges with complete hope and acceptance encourages me to face my own with a faithful heart.

I urge you to look for the people around you who display unshakable hope amidst their troubles—

especially children. Watch them, learn from them, and you, too, will discover that in every form of darkness, there is always light.

DON'T OVERTHINK IT

For a child, it is in the simplicity of play that the complexity of life is sorted like puzzle pieces joined together to make sense of the world.

—L.R. Knost

A question I ask kids almost ten times a day is, "What are you thinking?" It can be when we're on a walk, when they get up from a nap, or simply sitting at the table. I get so curious about what bounces around their brains in the most random moments.

One memory that comes to mind is sitting on the porch with Finley, a three-year-old with a wild imagination. I gave her a pencil and paper to see what her mind might come up with that day. She hadn't the slightest idea of how to even spell the word "plan," let alone write in complete sentences. She simply drew tiny squiggles and dots on the page while rambling for an entire minute about what each scribble meant.

In Finley's world:

= First, we can make pancakes.

= Then, we can do a craft

• = Finally, we'll end the day with a "sleepover" (which, in her mind, lasts the entire day), have a dance party, watch a "moobie," go to the playground, then play Barbie dreamhouse.

It's fascinating to me that her pencil can make one simple dot that, to her, represents every thought in her head. She doesn't overthink, edit, or erase what she desires in the moment. She simply conjures an idea, and she rolls with it.

It's become so common for us to overanalyze the decisions we make throughout our day. Choosing an outfit, deciding on a restaurant, heck even picking out a candy bar can be stressful! In today's world, we're bombarded with infinite options, each one seemingly better or completely different than the next. We spend more time worrying about the choices we make than we do actually enjoying them.

My close friends joke that asking me to make a split-second decision is like waiting for the grass to grow—don't expect it to be quick. You might have heard the saying, "those who overthink, overlove." So if you're a fellow overthinker, just know that it's a heck of a lot better to have an excess of love than a mind free of concern. And while a mind that overthinks can bring with it a steady stream of anxiety, there are ways to silence the inner critic.

Every time I start to spiral over a decision, I think of the way Finley described what she wanted that day—straightforward and to the point. Try to recall a time when you stressed out over a small decision. The next time you're presented with options, put on your blinders and go with your gut, despite what others may think. Do this, and it becomes impossible to overthink.

MAGIC

But leave us some magic in the world.
Leave us some mystery to enjoy.

—Stuart Hill

While reading a children's book about Easter, Finley, a three-year-old, looks at me and says, "Aria, I miss God." I was shocked by her response.

"He's with you all the time, Finley," I said. "You don't need to miss him."

"Aria, is God magic?" she asked. It didn't take her long to realize that she already knew the answer. She could feel it. As tears filled my eyes, I gazed into hers as they lit up from her smile. She sighed. "I love him so much."

This is one of my favorite stories because the lesson behind it is something this world needs to be retaught. Children come into this world allowing themselves to soak up every ounce of love they can receive. You can see it in their constant demand for attention, their boisterous excitement, and especially in their tendency to snuggle or reach for your hand. They mirror our innermost wishes.

Children crave *love*. We all crave love. However, the difference between adults and children is this: children believe they are worthy of love, yet somewhere along the way, we have convinced ourselves otherwise.

If you asked me to define my idea of faith, I would say it's believing in magic. Not the magic that pulls rabbits out of hats or makes shiny coins disappear. The magic I'm talking about exists within us, and we all deserve to feel it. To me, magic is the belief that we're all worthy of giving and receiving love no matter if we're six years old or sixty years old. Through these stories and thousands more, I've realized that to love a child, you must first love yourself. To truly listen to a child's thoughts, you must first learn to hear your own. Tending to a child's pain with empathy and compassion doesn't work unless you fully nurture care and compassion for yourself. If I'm able to voice to a child all the beauty they embody, then I must believe the same about myself.

My work with children has shown me the boundlessness of love. If I can see myself in a child, and teach them to live and love without fear, then I can do the same for myself. At the end of each day, if all I leave these children with is the memory of being loved, I've done my job. Now, my mission is to take the life-changing lessons they have taught me and continuously apply them in my adult life.

Learning to love is never-ending work, but if you take nothing else from this book, remember this: children exist to remind us that no matter what happens in life, we're here to love and to be loved. In other words… we're here to enjoy the small magic.

FINAL THOUGHTS

When deciding on the overarching message of this book, I considered the numerous family and parenting books I've seen and read from every bookstore I've walked into. And while each of these books contain hundreds of invaluable lessons we can teach children, I have yet to see a book that talks about what adults can learn from children.

My experience as a full-time nanny has changed my life in more ways than I ever thought possible. With each giggle, hug, and tear, it becomes even more clear to me that I've found my true purpose in this life. Being surrounded by children every day has opened my eyes to a world I once knew—a world where pancakes taste like candy and playing in the rain feels like you're getting away with something. Children awaken the innate part of us that knows what it's like to dream too big and worry too small, two outlooks that warp as we grow into adulthood.

Working with children for the past ten years has continuously reminded me that curiosity and creativity are two of the greatest gifts we're ever given, but the way that we harness these gifts will define who we become. I've found that the more time I spend with children, the closer I get to the person I long to be. I smile more, laugh at the littlest things, and—like most children—I don't focus on what others think of me. I'm completely myself. While my role as a nanny is to support, nurture, and care for these children, I've found that they're the true teachers when it comes to happiness. The adult world has so much to gain from the sympathy, kindness, and originality that blossoms inside the soul of a child.

My sincerest wish for this book is that it can serve to help adults unlock the treasure within themselves they once held as children. And even though some days (well, most days) their imaginations get them into trouble, by observing the ways children grasp the world, we might just find the clues we need to live an extraordinary life.

ACKNOWLEDGEMENTS

I would like to express my heartfelt gratitude to the following individuals who have played a significant role in the creation and completion of this book. Without their support, guidance, and inspiration, this project would not have been possible.

First, I would like to thank Hannah Kates, my exceptional editor. Your keen eye for detail, insightful feedback, and unwavering dedication to this book have truly elevated it to new heights. Our first encounter was most definitely written in the stars. Your expertise and professionalism have been invaluable, and I am incredibly grateful for your contributions.

To Andy Meaden, the talented designer who brought this manuscript to life. Your creativity, flexibility, and attention to detail have made the pages of this book better than I could have imagined. Thank you for your remarkable work and for turning my words into a visual masterpiece.

To the families who have entrusted me with the care of their children, I am deeply honored. It has been an incredible privilege to get to know and care for your little ones. Your trust and confidence have meant the world to me, and I am forever grateful for the opportunity to be a part of their lives.

Mom, your unwavering love, and support has sustained me through every step of the writing process. Thank you for your endless encouragement and belief in my ability to share this message with the world.

To my soon to be husband Ryan, thank you for always being there to listen to my endless trains of thought. Your patience and joyful spirit have been a constant source of strength.

To Brittany Joseph, the first mother who took a chance on a twelve-year-old girl with a dream of being surrounded by babies, I owe you a piece of this achievement. Your belief in me and the opportunities you provided ignited my passion and set me on this incredible path. Thank you, forever.

Lastly, but certainly not least, I want to express my deepest gratitude to all the children who have been a part of my journey. This book is dedicated to you. Your infectious laughter, boundless curiosity and unshakable spirit have enriched my life beyond measure. You have given me a source of joy I never would have otherwise known, and for that, I am eternally grateful. Please always remember the magic that resides within you.

In closing, I want to thank everyone who has supported me, directly or indirectly in the creation of this book. Your words of encouragement have made this dream a reality. Together, we have created something truly magical. Thank you.

ABOUT THE AUTHOR

Maria Horrigan is a passionate advocate for early childhood education, an experienced nanny, and a spirited traveler. Maria's commitment to nurturing young minds has led her to pursue a Master's degree in Teaching Elementary Education, which she will be completing in the spring of 2024. Her studies, in combination with her insights from her extensive travels caring for children across the country, have equipped her with a deep understanding of child psychology, educational methodologies, and the importance of play in fostering growth and development. She aims to make a positive and lasting impact on the lives of children and her future students, empowering them to unlock their full potential and to always reach for the stars.

www.ingramcontent.com/pod-product-compliance
Lightning Source LLC
Chambersburg PA
CBHW051546120626
46551CB00013B/1386